Ride My River With Me

Margaret Paige

HighLighter, Inc.
Fleming, Colorado

© 1987, by
MARGARET PAIGE

RIDE MY RIVER WITH ME (First Edition). Copyright 1987.

ISBN 0-940129-07-8

HighLighter, Inc.
Box 288
Fleming, CO 80728

PRINTED IN THE UNITED STATES OF AMERICA

What Does It Take?

How many days must pass on by
with parching heat of constant sun?
How many clouds must gather black
before our rainy season comes?
How many ponds will crackle dry
where herds of cattle used to drink?
Who can tell the farmer why?
How many years in torment spent,
births deforming, health denying,
poor neglected, children crying,
loving, loathing, trying, failing,
desperation, fighting, slaying?
There must somewhere be an answer.
What does it take
to make us care enough
to give ourselves in trying?

Introduction

I'm 88 and wheel chair bound;
so my days are filled with memories,
brightened by the glorious
river/mountain view that fills
my picture windows, and blessed
by the presence of the many loves
of my life. All of these precious
things I share with you.

Margaret Paige
Pueblo, Colorado 1987

CONTENTS

People
Old
and
Young

Taos Leather

The skin upon her bony arms
Hangs loose but tough enough
To wrap around them twice, she is so thin.
Eagle fierce are her faded eyes, deep set
But just as keen as they ever were.
They bore far through the winter shine
And seem to pierce into the depths
Of mountains far and blue where rest
The bones of ancient tribes unrecorded
But not forgot. They sing their tales
In chants that breathe over all their lands.
From sea across the plains
To the brooding heights
Of the great San Juans, their history
Is recorded on the remembering leather
Of that wrap-around hide.
She cannot die
Until her Phoenix memories
Are known and honored
Throughout her native land.

The Lucky Tramp

There was a man that I once knew
who was a tramp. He was never known
to sleep in a clean man's bed, or in
a woman's either, which might have
been much better, but he was foul of smell.
It was said he was afraid
of water and never took a bath at all.
He claimed to have some brothers but
they never claimed him back. So it
was thought that only animals would be
his friends and he was said to live with
them. Then later someone saw him
bathing in a stream with the animals
and it was thought they pushed him in.
After that the years passed by and he
was discovered, when quite old, sitting
in a rocking chair with a cluster
of kids playing around and an
adoring fattish little wife cooking up
a storm for them. She owned a
tidy little farm and was a thrifty
lady whose cooking spread the
smell of ham and beans and spicy
fragrance of her baking in the air.
Lured by it, many a tramp chopped wood
for her, then sat down on her stoop to eat
a bowl of tasty stew with other
things as well. But the master of
the house stayed strictly out of sight.
He'd had enough of dirt to add a
field to the farm of his roley poley
little wife, and didn't want to be
reminded of his hobo days.
If there's a moral to this tale,
it might be this: Be good to every
animal that you meet. You might
just need to live with them
some day.

They Gave Their Best at Lent

An uninspiring Rector
of a staid old church
pleaded for more money
to run his numerous operations.
He seemed to think the God
of all of them was money.
A fine plan reached his searching mind.
He asked that for their sacrifice
at Lent, they give up
what they cared for most.
A couple, faithful members
for more years than they could count,
walked away and agreed
with almost no argument.
They gave up what till lately
they had valued most.
They gave up the church.
The last I heard
they had not been back since.

Toothless Misery

My mother blamed me
for her toothless state, but I was toothless, too,
before I was even born.
I stayed inside her till I was fourteen pounds.
She like to not got rid of me at all.
She never gave me any teeth,
I had to grow my own.
My wife got turned off by my snaggle teeth
and threw me out after we had had
a toothless child ourselves.
She said it was my fault.
I'd rather gum my food
from birth to death
and marry me a gummer too
than have this fight
go on and on
forever more.

"I Have a Great Respect for You."

This was lately said to a young woman suddenly left with two tiny children to support after the sudden death of a brilliant and loving young husband just elevated to a position of trust and future growth. The smart little wife had used her brains and started a cottage industry, using her own home-making skills so she could support her children and keep them right there too. She was helped almost to their limit by both sets of parents, but soon decided she must make it further on her own. She was cheerful and sunny in her stance, and coming here one day bumped into this old gentleman in my home. They seemed to know about each other so I left them talking and picked up something else to do. He had quietly pressed her to let him help. He has long been alone with more income than he needs for his own wants, and he had similarly helped many others too. I heard a sudden gasp and turned to see the little lady holding him around the ribs and trying not to cry. It was just after he had said he respected her. I don't know what happened after this though I wished that I could pry it out of one of them. She left with a shining face, and he came back in, and sat silent for a few minutes.

"She's got a lot of loving going for her," he said, "but she seems to think she's too short and not too good looking either. I'll bet her husband thought she was something, and I do too! I guess she just needed to know how much respect she has earned as well".

The Eyes of Youth

Sweet sky and sun that seem
to reach through covering
of stern belief holding youth
to black or white or sometimes
gray of doubt. Unlock his mind
to find its own young simple way.
His genes are good, his aims
are high, he needs to be released
to try, and if he falls,
it only adds to his resolve
to try again. Some say
it is our failures that teach us
to be strong. I only know
there is a special haunting look
of dreams in his young eyes,
a straightened back of courage
and grip of reason in his hands.
He will do well
if he can make more choices
on his own.

I Talk to You

I talk to you, young friend, and you listen, for you
were brought up to believe the old
are wise and you can learn from them.
I thought so too, when I was young
and longed to make myself admired
for that great wisdom that automatically
fell from the lips of ancients.
Have you not witnessed the decay
that reduces centuries of stone and bone
to piles of rubble washed away by rains
and soaked into layers of the soil
that are o'er-laid by dust and volcanic ash?
Go listen to the voices of the earth
that knows all things yet does not
talk of them. 'Tis better that I
listen to you, so young, unspoiled,
unheard, and yet open to voices
even from within yourself.
You with the haunting eagerness
of eyes, teach me instead
to be new and wise
as you are now.

New Family

It is not blackness now
that drags my spirit down,
for that has mellowed to a rich brown
garment of acceptance that moves
around with me. Resolved to follow
with myself the tragic death
of the last and youngest brother,
almost my twin in tenderness
we felt one for the other,
something struck me desperately
awake. My tribe must not so vanish
from this earth.
So was I pulled back to sanity again.
Now June the second of this year
I will be the last generic member
of my clan for quarter of a century.
There must be a serious reason
for my living on so long.
Why should I not draw
together the ones of other families
so reduced, and form
a fresh new tribe? Why not?
Can you suggest a better plan?

Her Name Is Indefatigable

My next door, almost relative
is the workingest lady
I ever knew.
She grubs the weeds out
and braces up the plants
that after that, waver in their standing
till they become more independent
from support of friendly weeds.
The purslaine that she gathers
and brings in to me
gives bit of tang to salads
more nutritious and tasty then.
All can be hoed out and yet
new seeding comes next year.
The lady never knows it's time to stop, but going in for coffee
break or lemonade, comes out
again till exhaustion takes her
back inside to do the home work
after that.
What is this lady made of?
Work and sense of duty, beauty,
love of land and all its growing things,
but most of all a passion
for doing, teaching, growing, loving.
There is no end to her resolve,
or tender care for anyone in need.

Babysitting Grandma

I love you atrociosly, voraciously
And any old way you want it to be,
You little pet left here in my care.
You reverse the action and paddle me too.
I say outlandish things to you
When we are laughing, we silly two.
I hold between my fingers your nose,
Pretend to transfer it to your toes
And after that I put you to bed.
You're all worn out and I'm half dead.
I'll go to sleep immediately,
I hope we both sleep endlessly.
I'll gain the energy for this chore
It's only a day and a night, no more.

Hermit

A hermit living in a cave nearby
Became addicted to his pork and beans
And drove his donkey cart to town for food
To get him through the coming winter cold.
A buxom lady did entice him there
With whiskey and the smell of perfumed hair.
She threw him out in just his underwear
Dead broke and what was worse, sans pork and beans.

Nativity Scene

Here son, just say your piece again, and stand still! You sure you're going to be a saint this year? Last year you were a curly headed angel and tangled with another in the air. Sure you were just fixing that gal's halo and knocked it off instead of straightening it. You kicked the lantern over in the hay and darn near burned the whole place down. The year before you were a shepherd's boy holding your old hound dog a-licking everyone. Hank broke loose and slobbered on the baby and tried to climb right in the manger, too. It ended with you sitting on a box outside and holding Hank to keep the strays away. Now that was a good job you did last year. Why don't you ask to be a special guard outside the door this year and be the first one ever to guide the Wise Men in? Why are you scratching yourself, son? What is wrong? My God! You've got a fever and are all broke out! Now that's not good—but yet it's not too bad! Your mother might just keep you home in bed!

Blind

He who sits quiet there in his window chair, though he is blind, seems not to be restricted in his sight so vivid have his other senses grown. Experiences too, from his early sighted years now yield unending memories that are called out by hearing, smell and touch. He lies again beneath the aromatic pines with patches of blue sky above. Cries of animals far off or snufflings near reveal the humanness of creatures other than ourselves. Peltings by the pine cones seemingly thrown down by scolding blue jays, fail to intimidate the smaller birds that joyously do twitter their own songs of life and love. The prairies are recalled to which he clung when he was young, spread eagled on his belly, smelling earth and speaking with the crawling things and high behind small lumbering bugs. These long stored memories now vividly return and charge him with fresh energy and love of living, and those good souls who do for him the few things that he needs are drawn away from sorrowing for him. They are enabled and inspired to better live that they may serve their fellow men as he has more enormously done since he has lost his sight.

A Scholar and a Gentleman

He is a man, a gentle one
Yet strong as granite boulder
Sitting on the hillside near,
He does not know how good he is inside
Or how the others down below
View his stature as a man.
He is the last to see himself
As resolute inside, more understanding
Of the weak and damaged ones
That reach for his strong hand.
He must be told what others think
Whom he has rescued from the brink
Of suicide itself.
What can we do for such a one
Who will not hear
What others think of him?
I'm thankful that his home is next to mine.

Young Waiters

My friend was honored with a dinner
in the finest banquet hall
in the capitol of our state.
She sat at speaker's table
and I sat with others
of five hundred guests.
The tour de force was lobster tail
which I had seen
but never wrestled with.
I watched to see what others did.
They were either casual and too far off to see,
or clumsy and hesitated too.
A young man waiter standing near
spoke softly in my ear;
"Miss, may I help you do your lobster"?
He took my plate
upon his standing tray
and did the thing for me.
"It's quite a job. I butchered
many lobster tails before I learned
The Trick." The others watching
thanked him too. It was a lesson
from a gentle man.

A "Guest" Takes Care of Everything

Ray is a doer of all kinds of things
A picker upper, opener of cans and bottles,
Packages of airless cereal and finder
Of most everything that's lost.
He disappears when all is done, goes on downstairs,
Comes back upstairs when strangers come.
The vacuum drones, he's there alone
So looks for chores of any kind to do.
Shops for groceries, then declares
Things don't cost anything up here.
He goes all round and out of town
To find a frig for poor old Val
Who gets so hot she needs the most
Some ice at least to save her soul
Or disposition and finally, her self-control.
I hesitate to praise him more.
In truth it is not praise I seek
But just the simple honest truth.
For after all is said and done
What better word can I spread round:
"Diogenes has now been found."
A knight in slacks and sleeveless shirt,
A Socrates in quiet garb.
Pianist, producer, charmer, inducer,
Talent running out his ears, poetry dropping
From his tongue, charmer of the ladies
And pursuader of the raiders that seek
To desolate and rob us all of decency and honor.
Oh I could go on forever if I didn't get so
Wrought up that my poor old dilapidated system
Flares up and sends me stumbling off to bed.
A period is my ending now.

Talent

I could not have dreamed in that now
ancient time that you who came in my
studio door with eagerness but timidity too,
would grow to be what now you mean
to me. You touched me with your
frightened trying. I was humbled too,
as time went on, at each lesson's
growing sense of touch and talent
so intense with yearning
for the glorious sound that could
be lured out of my Knabe, still
my companion after fifty seven years.
You grew in every goodly way
as though spiritually led, and finally
took off on your own and I was
sorrowful but glad for you and others
to whom you have given more than
you received from me.
There seems no end to what your
giving of yourself will create.
It is a pebble dropped in the middle
of an earth sized lake.
Of such as you there can never
be an end.

Ultra Highs

Power and wealth were my inheritance
or so I felt when I was
old enough to think at all.
Why should I work to excel
in ordinary things?
So did I cruise along with others
of my style and class for half
a life time when dwindling
interest introduced the ultra highs of drugs.
Now drawing to the last gasp of
desperation, I am sick of life.
If I could once again walk erect,
an independent man, I would
grab at help of any kind.
Is it now too late for me?

14

Another Kind of Discipline

A small boy home from school rushed in the door
to find his mother sitting in her favorite chair
as if just waiting for his account of the day's
happenings. It came out fast, some things good
and some that angered him. She listened to all
with little comment needed. The child had dropped
his jacket on the floor and she seemed to take no
notice of it, but when he went to the kitchen for
his snack waiting there, he swung around,
"Was that you crying, Mom? What's the matter?"
Her face was still serene. "Oh, did you hear
that too? It must have been your jacket crying."
"Oh, Mom, I forgot."
He hung it up and ran out to the kitchen again.
No other word was said.

Rendezvous

The stars look in upon our rendezvous
And sparkle at the things they cannot do.
Complaints have come to us upon the breeze
That tattles back the fun that it has seen.
It matters not at all what's seen or said
My star is rocking in her water bed.
I watch her as she sleeps, she's only two,
And this is where we hold our rendezvous.

Perfection

"You're afraid you won't be perfect."
I'm afraid you'll think you are.
What would others have to be
to live up to your expectancy?
The narrow rim you'd have to walk
is far too sharp for me.
I'll drop back down into a warmer neighborhood
of sinners such as me.
It is a genial atmosphere
of helping other sinners
to be the best in their humanity.
Who needs perfection
if there be gentleness
and quick and kind
accessibility?

A Friend Reveals Her Secret

A friend, bright, energetic and witty
With black shining eyes and hair
Has a figure coveted by women
Half her age, and draws more
Than a second look from many men.
She had reared five good children
And now has seven living
Grandchildren as well.
An admiring friend asked her this:
"How do you eat everything
And all you want
Without getting fat; work hard
Twelve hours a day
And sometimes go out dancing
On week ends too?"
Her instant reply:
"Years ago I did try dieting once,
I gave up eating and kissing then.
It was the worst half hour
I ever spent
In all my life!"

Animals
and
Insects

Flora Flick

If you have thought
That a woodland tick
Just hides and sits
And painlessly chews
I hope you'll read
This tale I've writ
About a tick
That was in the news.

Perhaps you've heard
Of Flora Flick
Who lived right near
A fertile bog.
She went a fishing there
One day,
Sat down upon a tick
Asleep upon a woodside log.
He stuck her most ferociously;
She blew up like a big balloon
And rose up in the sky so high
She nestled right against the moon.
I think she fell in love with him
And won't be coming back real soon.

Breakfast with a Fly

Fly stuck in the last spoonful
of the special cherry jam
upon my breakfast toast,
I am angry and almost
fold you into squashing
but quickly change my mind.
It is ruin to my breakfast
and death to you as well.
You may be as hungry as I
but surely less intelligent.
I spoon you carefully from my toast
and stand you in a pie pan
with shallow covering of warm water
to wash your feet
and wadded bit of rag
to wipe them on,
then put you out
on my front porch.
Returned to toast and cherry jam
miraculously saved,
that tastes even better now
since your nuisance of a life
is also spared for a longer time.
Happy Valentine's Day
You fly!

The Hawk

Hawk with prey dangling from one claw
You have just flown by my window
As you did yesterday, and now you land teetering
On the limb of a winter bare tree
And balanced with your wings
Settle down to rest.
Now I see it is your leg that dangles there
And I am filled with pity.
I would help you if I could,
But you seem to be at ease
And aerate your feathers and shake them out
Then search the ground and river shore below.
You will survive somehow,
Perhaps to amputate your own leg
Or heal it, who knows how?
But you will live free as long as you can,
And take what comes simply
As must have been the plan intended for us all.
You have instructed me today
In better ways of handling my own infirmities.
My tasks are simple and few
And I will direct my mind
In accordance with your teaching
And watch more carefully
For other lessons yet to come.

Honey Bee

Too long you waited old honey bee
The lightning's blasted your honey tree
The wind has blown you away on high
To live with others up in the sky.

Now treat the angels respectfully,
Don't bother them and don't get funny,
The golden flowers will put the shine
Of golden lights in golden honey.

Behave yourself, you'll have it cozy
Don't listen to Satan. He's just nosey.
Say "Yes, Sir" to God and "No" to Satan
And all of your life will turn out rosey.

Bird and Cat

You little bird sitting there
too near that taffy colored kitten
with slits where sky blue
eyes should be, he's not asleep.
He only waits for you.
I cannot warn you
from inside by my window.
Blurred with unblinking watch
my eyes close down
for rest and moistening
then look out again.
It is too late.
No bird nor kitten
can be seen
nor any feathers on the ground.
There's only hope.
I breathe again.
Don't ever trust a slit eyed cat.

Max

You long banana dog,
you drag your middle
almost on the ground.
Shining brown your coat
and black tipped are your ears.
Why are you threatening
in your bark, with tail
that wags a lie to it?
I do not trust
the innocent whiteness
of your teeth.
Does it hurt to be so short
when others are so tall?
And do you hide resentment
behind a wagging tail?
What can I believe,
the teeth or the tail?
Let us talk the matter over
sensibly. I will not reach
my hand to you
till you speak quietly,
come close and ask me to.

Fruit Flies

Fruit flies hover near my mouth
So I can't talk lest they be sucked in
To their death and my quick throwing up.
A fly is someone I can swat.
Mosquito sits and bores,
Succumbs to blow that bruises
Black and blue the hide,
But fruit flies are a different tribe
And tribulation.
I don't know what is wrong with me
That I attract such company.

Horse Fly

You can't ignore the spinning
past your ear of that big fly
that settles on the back of your buggy horse,
and poises for the stab
that reaches through to sucking depth.
Lean out before he settles down
and seize him in cupped hands
and shake the devil out of him
before he has a chance to bite.
Confused and dropped into the dust
of buggy wheels, if he's not trampled on
or run over, the dust will keep him
cleaning up his act
till you are half a mile away.
Then you can pull up chumily
and share a big long horse laugh
at the fly.

Generous Dog

Dog, my neighbor, I would talk to you.
You bark at me when I come near.
You turn away and run back home,
And yet you are a generous soul
And leave your gifts when I'm not here.
Those dead spots in my lawn
That later grew so thick and green
Were where you earlier sprayed your nitrogen
And fertilized our favorite places
Here and there with your depositings.
How can I thank you
If you only run away?
Did you espy the broom
I held behind my back today?
It was to sweep the leavings on my porch
Of my friends the birds
Out on the lawn as well.
I have no animals of my own
So all you neighbors help me out
In this rewarding way.

Rattlesnake Joe

Rattlesnake Joe claimed that he had picked up
Many snakes and popped their heads off
On a rock, even a rattler sometimes.
I don't know about that, but Bill saw him
Pop a garter snake's head off
Though he didn't think much of that.
A kid could do it just as well,
But no actual country boy would kill
Anything but rattlesnakes mostly,
And even they do good if they don't bite someone
Or the cows in the head when they are eating grass
And don't see them in time
Or hear them rattle.
Bill saw a rattler once partway down
The throat of a big old bull snake
Still rattling till it was choked off
By going farther down.
We respected those old bull snakes
And picked them up and put them in a gunny sack
If they went near the chicken house.
They just love eggs and baby chickens.
We'd haul them away out in the fields
To live on rats and mice and bugs
That ate up the crops.
I tell you when you mess with nature
You're in a lot of trouble
Getting rid of all the pests yourself!
But rattlesnakes - that's something else.

Dolly's Colt

Frisky colt just two weeks old
what you doin' kicking up your heels
in Mama's face?
She only nips you in the rear
so she can walk or trot ahead.
She's got no time to feed you now,
quit getting crosswise in her way.
She can't just stop any time you say
to let you suck.
Now you've done it, kid.
The boss has got you tied
and sitting in the buggy too,
and coaxes Mama on ahead
with flick of buggy whip.
She's got to earn your living, son,
and you're darned lucky
you came along
instead of staying in the barn,
alone.

Animals Are Such Nice People

Mostly this is true. Animals seem to
have a sense of justice, of mercy,
sometimes forgiveness, admiration,
anger yes, and other unhappy emotions
with varying degrees of intelligence.
Altogether they must be graded,
some of them as more equable and
easy to live with
than many humans are.
Man may be the most ferocious
destroyer of them all because of his
superior comprehension and
imagination. I would rather join
the animals in all this. They are
the lesser of the destroyers.
There seems to be no better
creed than this early teaching:
"Let him that is without sin
throw the first stone".

I've never seen an animal throw
a stone at all.

Meadow Lark

Meadow lark on that cedar post
Spilling out your curling melody
Into the air, sing on, sing on.
The sunshine lilt, once heard,
Can never be forgot.
You float your song for all the
World to hear and seem to
Take life as it comes. You build
Your nest upon the ground
Beneath a tuft of grass or shade
Of prairie flower, or in a cactus bush.
How simple is your trusting nature,
For predators, from crawlers
To the wily coyote and birds of prey
May destroy your nest
Or carry off your young.
You build again and yet again,
Returning to other slightly shaded spots
To sing your song of joy and hope
From other cedar posts, and all the
World responds to that captivating sound.
May your lilt of courage and of cheer
Never leave the country of the cactus
Or be forgotten by my prairie heart.

Flirting Bee

I smelled a flower
Disturbed a bee,
I need to know
I want to see
What happens there
So secretly
Between a flower
And a bee.
I know about
The animals
And birds are free
For all to see,
But what goes on
Between a flower
And tickle-footed
Honey bee
Is still a mystery
To stupid me.

Busy Bee

I was advised to get a job
and work as hard as does the bee.
I went to see him as he worked
and he did sting viciously.
Now I'm still lazy but alive
while he's committed suicide.

Coyote Training

A coyote runs along a ridge with
learning pups behind. She is beginning
their longer look for prey out on
the prairie. Mountains harbor
dangers that are fierce and feral.
It may be better that they learn
on smaller prey that burrow
in the ground for cooling
and protection. The coyote
is a master at the waiting
game, with stalker scent,
and fast running feet.
Coyotes travel far and easy
on the plains. They will do well
when they have learned
the twists and turns
of living on the open land.

Flicker Flying Through

A sharp crack on my corner window pane,
And feathery patch of soft grey feathers left,
Kept me in my chair from wheeling close just to see what had
become of him.
Birds had sometimes fluttered down our cliff
And out of sight, we never knowing if they had lived or died
And so I waited quietly.

It was a full grown flicker flying fast,
And cutting through our double window panes.
Soon he flew up in the honey locust tree nearby.
Resting for awhile in the warm sun,
He shook his feathers free and flew off strongly to wherever he
was going.

I felt all set up for my own day.
I have so many things to do before I go,
So I can't fly away with him just yet.

Spotted Mare

I broke a spotted mare when I was young
that was as wild as western natives ever come.
She was corraled till we became accustomed
to each other. She fought the bridle, bit and
saddle, so I rode her with a hackamore.
The gate was opened to the prairie and we shot out.
I hung on somehow while she bucked and ran
and pitched again and finally settled down
to an ambling walk. Nice, very easy
was her gait. I wiped my forehead on my sleeve,
patted her and sat relaxed.
Right then that sun fishing devil turned
upside down and threw me on a rock.
I never knew how long it was till I woke up.
That crazy nag was lipping wetly at my neck.
Was it curiosity? Or maybe pride
that she had got the best of me?
I'll never know, but there she stood.
I climbed back on at last and neither
of us said a word. She seemed to think
I was her equal then.
I learned another thing.
Never treat a spotted mare
like an animal.

Goodbye, Mosquito

If you, mosquito, stick out
your hungry tongue
through that window screen
one more time
where I sit close,
and buzz your anger
once again at me,
I'll flick my swatter
and off will come
your probe for food.
I hope before you starve
you'll tell me why you hunger so
to draw my special blood.
My skin lies leanly
right against the bone.
You would have found no blood at all,
But I resent your trying for it
anyway. Goodbye, and better hunting
in your insect Heaven,
If there is such a one.

Cat's Advice to a Kitten

A friend of a friend had two male cats
A grown one and a kitten.
The older cat, celebrating
The Christmas season,
Became aggressive
And tangled with the tree.
He was snatched out of it
And taken directly for the operation
It was hoped would curtail
His violence.
He came back home
Walking cautiously,
And was heard to say
To the kitten,
"You'd better stop fooling around
with that Christmas tree.
Just see what it did
to me!"

Ranch
Life

Let's Start From the Beginning

When I was but five the plain was my home
almost it was back when the buffalo roamed.
It changed as time passed and later became
the home of Black Angus cattle and raising of grain.
Now it's no longer the home of the wild.
It's been so improved it's most civilized.
Eighty years later I now have a hunger
to go back and live there, I'm getting no younger.
I want to go back to the unbroken prairie
and play with the animals, gentle and scary,
But what will I do when I get way out there,
with nothing to ride on but my old wheel chair?
So I have decided to write my own story
simple and honest and somewhat folklory.
Swallow a sedative
or just do without it.
Relax everybody
and read all about it.

Was Hanging Them Too Much?

I know today how horse thieves felt
when they were strung up by the neck.
For though I was not forced to go through this,
my neck today was stretched by weight
of nearly fifteen pounds of sand
that put me very soon to sleep.
When I awoke, gone was the tingling
in my finger tips, but oh the ache
of jaw, and if the tongue
had not been strictly kept
behind the clenching teeth, it might have
ended with the tip of it lying
in my wheel chair lap. I have a sympathetic
feel for those fellows in the hanging days.
I wonder if they ever left a bit off tongue
protesting on the ground.
Might not the noose have been
too high a price to pay
for rounding up sometimes
a bunch of wild cow ponies
on the loose?

Bert

Bert was a singing cowboy, a "natural" with the most mellow voice and quietly alluring personality that seemed to draw to listening even country critters, too. His big guitar was his most prized possession and he was said to play it even on his horse when he was trekking across country to another round up job. He was sent for to play and sing at dances, for that was all the music needed, but when he lived so long in our valley I used to sit in with the music making unless the piano was too much out of tune. Bert had an ear for music that was phenomenal but he could not read a note. I could play a tune strange to him and he'd fall in with the choicest variety of chords. He never admitted to making up his own songs, seeming to think it not worth mentioning, but in these days he would have been snapped up and featured publicly. With any hint of that, he'd simply disappear and couldn't be found.

My repertoire of songs and memories were enriched in ways so colorful and vast in railroad and cattle country lore that it remains a store for me to draw from when life in town seems dull. He was a good dancer I believe, for every movement on and off a horse of that tall lean body with almost straight down legs was easy as the running walk of his big bay. He was never known to be angry or greatly fretted over anything. He was more than competent at anything he did, but most at ease when he was singing and playing anywhere at all. He seemed to drift away at last out of my range of living and he met his end far too young, but left such a store of amazing tunes and words lingering in the memories of those who knew and heard him that it added a whole new dimension to our lives.

Sometimes I see and hear it all again:

The Strawberry Roan; Sun Fishin' Sam; Go Down Fighting, Kid; My Heart is Not For Sale; Mammy's Cookin' Pinto Beans; Pickle Juice; Bunkhouse Blues; Singin' Rails; Too Big Britches; Susie's Fit to Be Tied; Night Mare Hollow; Home on the Range; Railway to Heaven; Oh, Bury Me Not on the Lone Prairie; Train Robber's Complaint; Last Shoot Out; Spook's Run; He Never Done Nothin' Wrong But They Done Him In; It Ain't Gonna Last; I Loved You Too Much, Babe; Sorry's Not Enough; The Gone Corral; Last Roundup; and Here We Go Round Again. Yes, my good old singing friend, we must keep going round again lest all the choicest times so simple seeming and so touching warm drift away forever. As long as memory holds, a life never ends that spends itself in singing.

Gramma Grass

Simple hills, so round, so brown,
holding hands to form the boundary
of our ranching home,
you must be softly green
with all the rains that have kept coming
still in middle summertime.
There grows to seeding heads
the gramma grass,
best of cattle feed
in all the West.
My eyes are hungry for long view
of pastures stretching back
to mountains blue.
In dead of night
my homesick heart
yearns to come back home
to you.

Cow Country Morality

Barbed wire fence
Cedar posts
Twisted, broken
Sagging wire
Desiccated coyote
Head wired to cross beam
Of ten foot cedar gate posts,
Coyote's mangy carcass
Swings in the wind.
Was it to warn others
Of the clan?
Fence walks back
Across a ridge
Staples pulled out
Barbed wires still lying
On the ground.
Old car tracks
Empty brass casings
Of bullets around.
What animal was hunted?
In winter coyote hide
In summer a cow
Or yearling calf
Or hind legs only
With carcass left
Rotting in the sun.
Why does the coyote
Hang swinging there
And not the man
Instead?

My Dad and Flies

My dad did the milking when I was a kid
sitting on a two-by-four milk stool,
two short pieces nailed together like a T.
Flies were bad in the country
in the summertime and sometimes
swarming around the milk shed
one would plop in the milk pail.
The simplest thing to do was
to lift it out with a finger,
but he tried to let no one else know.
He maintained that germs all stuck
to the flies feet, and anyway
country flies were healthier than city flies
that walked all over the town garbage
which was dirtier. Anyway, we were
strong and well and my dad was healthier
than most any other man out there
and didn't worry at all about germs.

He lived till he was well up in his eighties.
It was old age that seemed to do him in
and not the flies at all.

Winter Wind

Winds of winter's breaking up, even in the
sheltered place of my home, played with the
shingles on my roof last night. There was the
clipping sound of bird feet in frolic or in
fear, or just a barely holding on to their
precarious perch. But I lay confidently in my
bed and conjured up my childhood memories
that filled our old ranch home again, a
family of seven with four boys sleeping
undisturbed through disasters worse than
this high wind could ever bring. There was a
snow with drift above the eaves of our old
house that after melting, formed a crust
that could be walked upon. Sections of
corrugated roofing tin made speedy sleds
that tore down into the field below. Hails
that broke windows on the West were stopped
with tacked in boards till later, sheets of
glass kept in our farm shops for such emergencies
could be cut, fitted, and puttied in. Large hay
stack canvasses made temporary roofs till
shingles could be brought out from town eighteen
miles away. Blizzards from the North overshot our
house, farm buildings and corrals, for they snugged
up against the highest range of gramma grass
hills that reached out protectingly on either side.

I was beguiled into remembering that early
home, and wrapped in all that love again,
pulled up the covers to my chin and
went to sleep.

Egg Frying Sun

When sun shone down with
hottest rays in middle summer
on the ranch, once in a while
work was called off earlier on
Saturday for oiling harness, greasing
wagons and cleaning up for
Sunday, and the following week.
Once in a while the boys would want to
cook our supper on the smooth flat
rocks out in the sun all day.
Everything required a lot of grease
and then the food would stick, but
dogs and cats and chickens picked them bare when they were
through
their cooking. Skillet bread was somewhat rubbery but tasted extra
good. Tea was made in jars of
water left in the sun for several hours.
The eggs were best of all reflecting back the orange gold
of deeper coloring in country things.
My recalling times grow ever
more explicit and comforting
as time rolls by.

Irrefutable Borders

"Eat something and lie down".
Those are my orders when I go too long
without food and a slight headache starts.
I told a young working friend this. He nodded
his head and laughed.
"That's good for people half your age,
but how do I convince my wife?" She says
"it's hotter standing over a cook stove.
At least there's fresher air outside."
I once knew a young fellow working
on a ranch to toughen up for the fall
football season. He gave completely
out, chopping weeds out between the beet
rows. He had been cautioned to go easy
for awhile but he had wanted to
prove himself. About two o'clock he
wilted and flopped down under a big
cottonwood tree and fell asleep.
When he woke up later, his boss
was sitting close and fanning both
of them with his straw hat.
"Well, son, I guess you needed
rest more than the beets need hoeing.
I brought a jug of lemonade for us
both and I've had mine. Just take
your time. It's hotter now than
when I first went down my row of beets".
There are certain times and people
that are indisputably good.

Home

Oh night time breeze that brings again the fragrance of my early prairie home where grew the gramma grass with sage and native flowers and animals of different species living as nature directed them. Are they still there?

Almost a century have I lived and for these many later years mixed have been the fear and longing to know what has happened to those clear days and breathing nights with view of Rocky Mountain Range threatening and protecting as the seasons rolled along.

Old ruts of covered wagon trails and deep-worn buffalo paths to water holes had grown visible with thicker growth of grass where rainwater had collected for deeper watering. The forgiveness of nature had restored the scars to greener covering and thicker sods that wasting winds could not blow away.

I wonder if there still come the sounds of insects, birds and animals in winter, summer, spring and fall. Are they heard as once they were?

There seems to come again in dead of night the yapping coyote chorus and smell of skunk adrift upon the air that carries it away. Sleep comes at last. May there be heard again the songs of mocking birds and meadowlarks each morning as I go along the never ending road of dreams ahead.

Arroyos

Arroyos have been my awesome dread
since I was five when I first stood
upon the bank of one and looked down.
I fell back sick and clinging to a tuft
of meadow grass, heaved up
my own small flood and was carried back
to the house a quarter mile away.
It hugged the upper range
of bounding hills of our valley
stretching forty miles to the foot
of old Pikes Peak. The roaring of the
waters could be heard above the other
ranching sounds, and I am dizzy
after all these years at the thought of it.
But now it brings a glow of ruggedness
and survival wish to live till someone
stops that gross destruction and waste.
Man has done far greater things
in the air and sky, and similar things
as this upon the earth, and harnessed
all that power for useful ends.
I cannot bear to die and miss all this.

Dude Ranch

The summer cowboy on the ranch
gets on his horse as he is taught
and gets off on the right. He has forgot.
Then seeking to redeem himself,
he gets back on again from the right
and then falls off the left. At any rate
he is now doing that maneuver right,
and takes a nip of refreshment from his hip.
His chaps, too hot in summer,
fan the breeze as he tries to imitate
the walk of cowmen, and wishes
that his legs were not so straight.
He clips the roadside weeds with his quirt,
and rowels of his spurs jingle as he walks
back to the lodge. The cowhands that
take care of him only glance at one another.
They earn a goodly wage
playing nursemaid
to the scared and swaggering
Riders of the Purple Sage.

Prairie Water Troughs

The windmill turns with creaking sound
as long as there is wind to turn it.
The cattle standing round the galvanized
troughs drink slow and long and
stand in the slopped over mud to
cool and soften their dried out hoofs.
They pull back to make room for
new ones coming in, and dally with
the weeds and shorter grass nearby.
A rider, coming from afar, is
heartened by the sight, and pats
the dried out water bag hanging on
his saddle horn. His horse,
smelling water steps up his gait.
The cows pull back a bit, then draw
near again. The cowman drinks
directly from the running spout and
dunks his head and face clear under.
His horse drinks long and steadily,
pauses, heaves his sides then
drinks again. He lips the water
playfully. The cows draw close
and stand at ease. There is no
enmity nor fear at water
troughs when prairie winds
turn water wheels
in summertime.

Zane Grey

Who were the Riders of the Purple Sage?
Any reader of the tales of the early West
could tell you who wrote those thrilling
stories of wild and woolly doings with
deadly adventures, a mix of violence,
stampeding herds, horse thieves hanged,
and men's early savagery and justice.
It was Zane Grey, of course.
But always weaving through the chicanery
and violence there was a golden thread of
honesty and virtue and a longing for
the good, and at the ending of each tale
the loving couple settled down on their
homestead content, or rode into the sunrise
of their dreams. There was a reaching out in
desperate need for religion too. Christmas
Eve was variously observed in a log cabin
church or in the bawdy towns with liquored
celebration or hoe down or raucous box
supper and dancing till a falling down
dawn put the celebrants to sleep. Oh, there
were hopes and dreams, too and Christmas
Day their version of the Nativity scene.
But what the first Magi carried on their
camels, gold, frankincense and myrrh was
more likely to appear on the backs of sure
footed mules across the Rockies by Riders
of the Purple Sage, with bags of gold dust,
casks of hope and flasks of mirth.
How can we, in all our dignity,
do essentially any better than that?

My Mother

"...Who Live In My Home Town."

My mother loved the song about the gentle people in my home town and sang bits of it under her breath. It was when she was getting weak and spoke softly too, as though her thoughts were inside and private.

It embarrassed me for it brought tears to my heart and eyes. There had been so many times when it hadn't been so good for her and sometimes my inside angers had spilled out with the wrong sound but I could never tell her that.

And now I am as old as she was then and there are gentle people in my home town too. I can not now remember the angry words that others may have said to me when they were young and hurting and didn't know why.

So now I cry again in the forgiving of myself at last. I wonder if she knows.

Dad and the Steer

My Dad rode out one day to look over the yearling calves pastured near the house on a harvested field with better feed before the winter snows would cover it. One steer had crawled through the fence into an adjacent field and Dad hoped to rope him and drag him back. He tied the end of the rope to his pommel to secure the animal if he should break and run and miraculously dropped the loop over his head. The calf was jerked off his feet and Dad's thumb, caught in an unexpected loop, was jerked off at the joint with several inches of tendon attached to it, we later learned. He somehow loosed the steer, and holding his wadded bandana over his hand hurried in and called to me to bring a big clean cloth and the iodine. I followed him behind the house. "I don't want Mama to know about this," he said. I soaked the rag with iodine and he slapped it on the wound, turning his back so I could not see. He gave a few low howls of pain before the anesthetic action settled in. Thirty miles and two hours later at his office where my brother had driven Dad, our doctor cut the bone off shorter to get more flesh and skin to make a padded stump for greater comfort and usefulness. Dad never complained and did almost everything he had done before and it was good. One thing he could not do was to fasten his starched collars over the tiny collar button when he dressed up to go to town or to our country Sunday School where he was the Superintendent. Mother always helped with his collars. He never liked to talk about his accident and I don't remember Mother ever chiding him about the mistake he had made. It was the breaking of a long established custom in our home. He had ridden out and done unnecessary work on the Sabbath Day.

The postlude to this story came that same afternoon before we heard what had really happened. A blundering old fellow who was working for us then, walked out and searched the field and found my father's thumb and held it out to Mother.

"I found Mr. Paige's thumb and I thought you'd like to have it."

"Oh, mercy, he didn't lose his thumb, I know it's not that bad!"

"Oh yes, ma'am, it's his thumb all right. I thought you'd like to have it."

"Oh Heavens, oh no! Oh please!"

"Well then, can I have it?"

"For mercy sake, what for? On no, please! What would you want it for?"

"I thought I'd just like to have it to remember Mr. Paige."

Someone intervened and later quietly buried it.

Now seventy years later a curious thought occurs to me. The only personal thing of our large family's more than sixty years of living on that cattle ranch is resting there, that small bit of us. My Dad with his chuckling sense of humor might well have enjoyed this true and earthy tale.

Farm Hands From Town

Experienced hands out on my brother's farm
in haying time, drank water
from canvas water bags,
wet frequently on the outside
and hung on nearby limbs
or in any other shade.
One city boy, although warned,
insisted on taking his own water pail,
chiefly chunks of ice chipped off
the blocks in our big ice box.
He collapsed with misery and
the shakes, insisted on wobbling in
by himself to lie down and be
cared for by my mother.
So did he learn, and other too.
By summer's end he was stout
and bronzed, at least twice the man
he was. Vic called these boys
his kindergarten, but never in their hearing.
He loved them and he was strict.
When they went home
their families were amazed at their
lean hardness, white teeth shining
in brown grins they never needed to
brag about any time.

Scotty

Scotty was a flaming sorrel stallion bought by my adopted grandfather, an aristocratic Englishman who had migrated when he was twenty to America's Democracy and thrill of living in our eighteen seventy West. Many years later, his Titian haired spirited daughter, Mary, saw and coveted the stallion and Chumley bought the horse for her, but spent some time first in taming him. He felt he must make sure he would not pursue a mare if there was a rider on her, perhaps a child, so he devised a plan. Loading a double barreled muzzle loading shotgun with lesser amount of power, he used instead of shot a load of hard dried beans, and rode out through the pasture where Scotty ran loose with other mares. His mount was a sweet grey mare he kept for his special riding ease, not yet acquainted with young Scott. When she was sensed, the stallion pounded hard toward her and just as he rose on his hind legs, Chumley let him have the charge of beans right in his chest. He instantly dropped to his feet, shaking his head and mane in anger and bewilderment. A little later Chumley rode near again and Scott pursued, but with less speed and when Chumley lifted the gun, he turned at once and thereafter looked, but pretended to be indifferent. Only a raised arm was needed now and then. He seemed to be almost human in his sense and memory.

Mary and he had many a battle for supremacy, but it became a love affair until she met and married a young Yale professor and moved East for good. Before that a few times, when Mary was away in school, Chumley would ride him the two miles to our ranch and boosting me upon young Scotty's back visit with my parents while I rode for several miles of thrill that was the greatest I ever had with horse. The movement of his striding power was indescribable except to say it was like riding on the wind.

I was ten years old at that time.

My Mother's Rocking Chair

My shoulder blades lean back to soak up the heat of setting sun and head pulls up straighter too. It is the same old country heat as in my youth. My mother's rocking chair sits facing me, ready to visit with my old wheel chair. Its back shines with orange lights and deeper hues in the brilliant sun. The arm rests, shaped for tiredness, are polished to silkiness and I see those wondrous working hands resting there or folded in her lap for a little while before she went to bed. She would lean back and sometimes when she closed her eyes she seemed to be lost in prayer or reverie. I wonder now how she could live so calmly through those tough and tragic times interspersed with homely warmth and precious stroking of quietness and love. I visit with her often as she rocks so gently, or just leans back and rests. She lived till she was almost ninety-one. She has not seemed to die at all.

Earth
and
Life Upon It

White Footed Clouds

White footed clouds,
You tread so lightly
Along the far line of hills
As if caressing them to sleep.
Wake them up with greenness
Once again, after you
Have drenched them
With abundant rain.
The cattle feeding there
Upon the browning gramma grass
Will languish
As the other animals do
When the source
Of all their nourishment
Dries up.
I will lie down in quietness
To listen to the sounds of storm
And may there be
Renewal for us all
When morning comes again.

Walking Trails

The cattle trails of long ago
have been demolished
by the trespass of human beings,
and bridle trails took over
what was once wilderness.
This is a pleasantly natural use.
Now another population growth
demands bicycle and walking trails.
Those two have added to the nature walks
that benefit both old and young
but must there be a deluge
of beer cans strewn along the way
and fast food bags thrown in the woods
or impaled upon the bushes
along the side?
And what of sites demolished,
seats and tables broken or set on fire?
What have we so-called human beings done?
The old time animal trails
were cleaner than are some of ours
today.

Fall in July?

You Fall, now in the middle
of July, why do you
disturb us now
to wanting you to stay?
It cannot be, although most pleasing
to us, sweltering yesterday
and earlier days.
How would you handle
all the growing, ripening, curing
that must be done before freezing
takes over once again?
Oh, no! Don't leave us so soon!
A few more days and nights
of utter bliss before we wrestle
in our sweating beds
and fight to get the best
of summer heat again.

Watermelon Squash

You strange big watermelon
or striped squash,
not hard and shining
but softer as a squash in heat.
You grew from seeds
that rotted in your garbage heap
and spawned a strange
and unknown treat
or horror, who can tell?
You have a watermelon's curl
green now but later black
to tell it's ripening.
A giant will you likely be
with food from such fertility.
My greatest hope that you
will be both edible
and delectable.

First Freeze

Last night a hard freeze laid our garden low, and when the morning came the vegetables were limply draped along the rows or on their mounds as though they wanted to go home into the earth from which they came. But suddenly as though with change of heart, it warmed up fast and sun shone hot and brassily down on fallen plants and almost glued them to the ground. But those old cottonwoods below just laughed out loud. It was what they had long been waiting for. So long in turning color, this cold slap to running sap, began to make it do its customary job of disappearing lest it be frozen too. At last the lagging trees returned to their fall duties, and gold and green the smaller things may now turn rust and red, and putting on their lesser but still appreciated show. Now once more challenge works anew. The fall performance will go on again; the trees and weeds, wild things and we will just enjoy and clap our hands and leaves together.

The Year's Full Circle

January seems the longest month of all and breathes down the neck of February that hurries March into spasmodic weather giving way at last to April's enigmatic vagaries.

Encouraging and freshening May leads warmly into June for existing of romance and growing of the earth and all things on it. June is hotly followed by July that steams itself into a sweating unpredictable fat August.

September's ripening lushness with mild cool weather gives out the bounty of air and field and stream and feeds or enriches all creatures and growing things around. Now October further ripens and stores up for leaner months the profligate supply of nourishment that should feed all the world with more even distribution.

November is the glory month of harvest and Thanksgiving with flaming colors in the dawning and the sunset skies that later variagates and deepens taste and color. These linger on into the frigid long December.

So do we come full circle again to Christmas time with the glow and meaning, variously but deeply felt communion with even those whom we may never know or understand. It does not matter if we never touch hands at all. We know that they are there and need us as we need them.

To that resolve on my own part I pledge my energies on this dim but now lightened day. It is heaven enough for me to have lived this long.

Winter

You beat your violent self against my double window pane that lets through just the crackle and the occasional creak of adjacent family woods. It is an uneasy and often violent assault and I would welcome a returning of your calmer self and a warmer coming in of our December. But now, fierce wind, you seem to have no heart at all for the hiding creatures of the wild.

The tree-rocked magpie's nests swing and sway. The winter staying mallards fly out and back in any wind. The shy small woodducks have gone away for feeding or their other enterprise. Bob Steel, with flown-in pairs, has brought the woodducks, once destroyed by hunters' guns, back to the home where once they thrived. Now they can be seen as they were then in all their brilliant elegance, in sleeping and grooming groups or swimming singly or in pairs in their preferred habitat. It is a thrilling and touching thing, and with beauty start and end my days, for they stay all winter long as mallards and other waterfowl do.

But for now they've gone for a bit, and the winds swings up and somewhat modifies its violence.

I forsee a milder and brighter tomorrow. May that be true for all of us who do what we can to bring in a better life for all, but most of all for those whom we try to help.

May it be a warmer and a brighter day for all of us.

Our Love Today

What will we create, or do, in this our only today? Haunted by this thought I wakened to look out on the falling snow that nudged the wakening Spring back to bed of Winter once more. Is it a respite for the motivation of the generative power that lives within all living things? Those beings who die in hope while they can still move about on their own are too much to carry - let them go. Count me not with them. Some task will walk in my open door to spark my spirit to new discovery. This quiet tells me so.

Tyrant, Day

The day got up with me at half past six or thereabout,
But it was later than was I who sat
Upon my bed to wait for energy to rise.
I slow and cautiously crept to my old wheel chair
And then the day found itself to be too slow
To keep up with my eighty-seven years, nine months,
The days and hours accelerating fast as one
Can think, the minutes, seconds, flying by
Swifter than thought. Now I'm upset. You scare
The Hell out of me, day. Get off my back!

The New Year

On the third day of this New Year, the dawn comes in with uncertain hues
of sage-grey, palest lemon, saffron, then holds it's breath awhile.

We wait with anxiety for your coming in, new day, for yesterday was too
much grief and trouble and should have been over-leaped.

Turn on your heat and bring up the sun with flame that turns the snow-
dressed peaks to fiery light of orange, reds, blues, purples, all colors
blending against the sky that fades into the distant blue of open day.

The disasters of yesterday grow dim as my spirit settles down within me
with quietness at last.

Now, infant day, my assumed responsibility I turn over to you. Take hold
of all. I tried to help too ardently and left in confusion and dismay. Run
things in your own way, you lusty three-day old, and I'll just sit here and
nap.

New Day and New Year

Settle down and take your seat now, eager day.

Your sun is up and moves its rays smoothly spreading warmth that makes the old earth yawn and stretch to limber up. The body that was inert the long night through requires a longer awakening time.

Your millenium of learning years has not yet reached maturity. So you go on and leave that knocking of the new young year unheard till you deliver up a better record of what you've done.

But I must tend to my own affairs. For this fine day may turn out to be the very best of all for me.

Morning Moist and Cool

Confidence comes in with coolness
as the sky and river meet
and moistly embrace.
A lone gentle breeze
disperses slightest fog
that drifts along.
It may be only felt and imagined
so quiet is it all.
New softness comes to skin.
Astonished are my fingers
at the feel of chair arms, table tops,
and even the paper on which I write.
Breathing comes easy.
Moisture, that flecks the patio
outside, comes in the window
changing everything since yesterday.
Now comes the easy spending
of a day, openhanded, leisurely.
The earth breathes in and out
as if we all were freshly young
again.

Lazy Day

Lazy kid of a day
You wake me up
at nine o'clock.
The rooster crowed
four hours ago
to get you up.
You opened bright
your sunny eye,
then turned me over
in my bed
and went to sleep
yourself again.
What have you done
to your own world
left to grope its way
in foggy rest?
I summon you
to open up the blinds
and bring yourself
into my little shack
or I'll bedevil you
lazy day
for all the time
you've made me lose.
I'm spinning on
to eighty nine.
Young fellow
I'll have to tell you
that you're fired!
Now after this
I'll get up
and going once again
all by myself.

Growing Up

It's time for you to walk alone today into the woods, my little one, that has so long been yours and mine together. We explored it all when you were small, astride my neck to reach the leaves and swinging vines, startling the small birds and following them with your eyes into the sky. A drift of clouds, snow white puffs were sailing there against the blue.

It was a wondering day for you and sweeter one for me. You walked then afterward all by yourself and ventured far ahead and learned, and I learned too the ways of boys like you. The forest taught us both, and all the creatures in it did for us the best they could, and even the inanimates spoke with us. We touched the smooth trees and the rougher bark, and pushed still farther into thick and taller stands of timber. There the moisture clung in mossy patches on the sides of trees and on the rocks that stood beside the streams that spoke most forcefully of all of their remote beginnings. It was such wisdom that we were breathless in our listening. But some brooks babbled on quite mindlessly we thought, but even they may do some good in passing on the news (or gossip) of the day. Thus they taught us independence and the need to choose the best of our humanity for our own deeper understanding. So it went for many conversations in those deep woods. Sometimes, later, in the winter time as you grew older, we would spend a day and night there learning from the wild ones how they stood the cold, the winds and snow. At night as we lay close together, we would test the tricks of keeping warm til daylight came and we could find our way back home. Your freezing hands sought your armpits and my own, and warmer were between our thighs, or both of ours together between mine. But now the day has come at last for you to walk your own new way, my great-grandson. If you look back you may not see me, but I'll be always there to wave you on. For now, at last, I must go deeper into my own woods, and lie down to rest.

Sunsets Must Be Free

"Sunsets are for all to enjoy." That is what
the city writer said. "Even our city treasures
must be shared with anyone."
A man needs most of all to own something
that is free to all but beckons personally just
to him. I was that man. We travelled
over all the country, sought out-of-the-way
places where quiet could be found, and
finally bought an isolated smaller cattle
ranch we could afford. It was a long
hard time of learning, but our neighbors
helped us, and trial and error taught
us sometimes disastrously, but we are
slowly making it at last. We fought with
winds to stand alone. The storms
swept fiercely over all the land.
I reached my dripping arms straight up
and dared the lightning to strike me down.
My soul was saturated with the glory
of standing on my piece of land. I had
earned my right to living here.
I have a stake in everything I see,
and sunsets now belong to me.

We Live Together

A great grey bowl floats loosely all along our undulating or roughly varied far horizon. It seems to draw its farness to within ten miles or less, and the near line of trees almost within my reaching hand. They put their arms around me and I smooth their leaves so cool and soft and invite them to lie down with me for closer intimacy with nature of which I am but one small part. You, leaves, are young and pliant and could yet ride the crest of rivers to explore the distant seas. Why not? I did it once in winter time and you are eighty-six years younger than am I. But now we must confer, old trees and I, to see what we can do to keep well fed and warm the creatures of the forests and the streams. We will speak too, with shrubs and smaller weeds and dormant seeds. The stolid rocks may break their centuries of silence and give to us their wisdom. Some tiny creatures have already tried to move inside with me to sleep within my deep shag rug and for their room and keep, eat up the bugs and moths and destructive insects, as well as crumbs and other particles of food. Just yesterday a tiny lizard waited near the side of my front door and quietly slipped inside, but Mary's broom swept him away. Too bad, my little love. Other ones have done the same in previous years, and staying in my bedroom, tried to sleep with me. Once there was a tiny one that ran across my face, scaring me awake. That one I hunted down a few days later and put into a hole where others lived beneath my outside cement stairway to the basement rooms below. But there are other tiny beings already inside with me. A cricket chirps astonishingly loud till he is found and ushered out, but spiders weave their webs courteously out of reach, and catch the lesser insects that still pester me. So do we altogether try to make it easier on all of us, and I like it just that way.

Rivers
Mountains
Plains

Lady River

Buxom lady river with undulating gait
sweeps round the bend from her clouded
virgin source to this elegance of maturity.
She has the dignity of a Dowager Queen.
Her gown flows majestically along
ruffled by the trailing of grass and shrubs
along the banks. Her innocence
still shows in the frothy white
of its churning across the rocks.
It is the trimming on the royal river gown.
This is for some a resting scene
but there are others who would choose
to lie upon the royal lady's crest
and float the length of her long journey
into the boundless sea.
How magnificent to ride along with her
and see things that other mortals
may not have known at all.
There are still dreams for future men
to bring into reality.

Flaming Sun

Fireball in the West
that cannot be looked upon
lest it be the last clear vision
of the marvels of the setting sun.
That flaming light
drops out of sight
yet still the heat of its burning
will warm the dark obscuring night,
and carry through to one more dawn
the glow of still another eager day.

Coming Rain

Only slightest lean of tufted grass
From East to West
Hints of moisture blowing in.
It promises relief
From scalding heat inside
Desert dryness on our hill.
West winds blow the wind away
But East winds give a whispering
Of hope that rain
Will begin at last
The earth sits open mouthed and waits.

Sun God

Sunbird sitting there on purple peak
beyond the reach of anything
but Eagle Eye through which your rays
light up the day, stay where you are.
You are too fulsome in the heated summer
and far too powerless in the ice
of winter time. Why must you change
so drastically, you who the ancients
thought divine? You are no Lord of Hosts,
for such as they control themselves
to set example for mankind.
Sometimes you seem a fancy devil
in golden light disguised.
I would that I could cast the devil
in you out. We need a Moses
once again to give us laws to live by
just as then.
Alas, poor Moses was not
listened to any more
than I am now.

Gold

The clouds of last night's storm
hang grey above the brown horizon.
The thin sun slices in between
with concentrated light
that flashes gold the symbol
on the farther church or mosque.
Is it a Cross, or Star of David,
or another sign of Oriental faith
or Majesty of thought?
If it leads us into harmony
and peace, does it truly matter
if each gets there his own way?

Heady Day

The wrestling rain and wind of yesterday
have fought each other to a draw.
Uncertainty died in the forgetting night.
Morning is born anew
with no remembrance
of what went on before.
The far off mountains, laced with snow
are bluer in the sun and nothing stirs.
Breathlessness becomes the newborn Spring.
The grass pricks up its tiny blades,
and near the rocks the heat of sun
brings into early blossoming
flowers that spread their fragrance
over all the plain.
There is a heady steam
of renewal in the air
as life begins again.

River Play

Down on the river bank below
a man above sits on a log
and bending over seems to play
with crawling things or colored stones
worn smooth with shine of water
in the sun. He turns and looking
up at me beckons me to join him
there. Floating down on morning
breeze we wade together in the stream.
As two small children once again we
laugh and play with pebbles and
our toes. We are creatures only of
the atmosphere, unseen
and I was well as he. Now he is
gone and I again sit quiet in my
rolling chair, but I feel now that
I, unbound, can fly at will most
anywhere I want to go.

The Great Divide

Viewed fresh and clean in morning light
the high ridged Great Divide thrusts up
its Rocky Mountain peaks and clefts
between the ridges purple now
against the blue morning sky.
The sun strikes out to fire the bald Pikes Peak
and dissipates its lighting down the slopes
now settling down to the quietness of day.
This is the jagged and oft meandering line
that divides our continent, East from West,
but must it so divide us all?
I wonder why the more brainy ones fight on
with others of our species
for what is plentiful for all
if we but cared enough for one another.
I wish sometimes that I could crawl
a-lumbering along with other bugs and
independent seeming things, and quiet live,
alert to those that seek us for their food and drink
but otherwise dwelling with the rest
of our dumb friends
in naturalness and peace.

Tornado Clouds

Rise up to overhanging
you white cloud growing.
Come near, grow dark,
gather together your blacker force.
We who stand here desolate
on our dry cracked land
must risk disasters.
When black clouds rise up
over mirage of desert heat,
then comes tornado power
and sucking sweep of hurricane.
Lightening just a little now,
give way, spread out
to drenching of wide falling rain.
God of Terror and of Storm,
let us take whatever comes
with thankful hearts.

Loss

The screaming wind
sinks down at last
wooing once again
back to quietness
the violence that had gone on
all day and night.
The creatures shake off
the litter of the storm's debris
and go about their living
as if it had not happened
at all.
But I cannot forget
the agony of my losing you
as once again your beloved voice
called my name upon the wind.
I cried out again and again
in answer to that tender call.
Only a sigh reached me
on the dying breeze
and that was all.
But young and ardent
once again
you live on
in the soul of me.

Red-eyed Sun

Red-eyed sun comes flaming up after a turgid and scarring night, black as a hangman's hood with darts of angry lightning through the blue-black lowering clouds.

There is not a living creature to be seen.

The mountain crest roars down its avalanche of snow and rocks and buries what no one will ever know until long months after the winter is put down and the slow-melt of snow spills out its icy flood over the spongy earth that tells the winter's tale that has been writ. This document adds thus another layer to the ancient register of eons since there was nothing at all, or so it is surmised by some.

Whence comes this vibrancy of life that shakes us once again with this new spring and how did we humans come in at all?

Theories vary and are thought true or false or lost in endless controversy.

I only know I am alive yet and overcome by that glorious fact. Whatever comes, leading beyond our thinking or our vision there lies a road that stretches out of sight ahead. I will go on along that road as long as I can.

Ride My River with Me

I do not need to travel far to see the world
or sense and hear and feel the marvels of the universe.
The view is limitless from out my cliffside window
looking steeply down into the growing Arkansas
fed by melting snows and shouting cataracts
from nearby Rocky Mountains. In my fancy
I am floating on the aspen leaves in summer
and the trees that are torn loose by wind and flood.
I ride on ice chunks in the winter, or swim underneath
with all the fishes. The beavers take me into their warm lodges
and I feed with them. On moonlit nights they float me on their logs
or launch me, ocean bound, toward warmer waters and the sea.
I become the guest of all the creatures of the streams and of
the shores,
and they are friendly and they nourish me with their best food,
and it is good. And I lie down with fiercest animal
and amphibian and am protected by them all.
When I become at last too tired - satiate and content,
I am returned somehow to my sweet Colorado home.
Awake at last, still sitting in my old wheel chair,
a new-born sun just gilds the tops of my beloved cottonwoods
and filters down to waken the wild ducks that sleep
in deeper and more quiet pools where they have always harbored.
Gloriously free they go through all their morning rites
quite unabashed,
for we are friends and lovers too. Then having fed
and groomed themselves and each other, I am rested too.
Am I really eighty-seven? It cannot be! I'm only twenty-three.
My heart beats hard, my breath comes fast, and suddenly
I'm young again, and I fly off with them into the sky.

Seasons of the Heart

A Galloping Horse is Today

Jump on behind, you who would ride with me,
or in front, for we ride bareback
in closer contact with our mount,
the source of energy between our legs.
No one can hold to slower gait
this glowing day that freshened
by two days of resting clouds and showers
on the upturned face of August
leaves the restless river dappled green
with algae through which the ducks
make streaks in patterns along the shore
as they chase each other with ardor
or with punishing intent. Must we remain
static in our watching? The road
along the bank is for our riding
and there will never be an end
to our racing river. We must make
the most of this pungent day, the only one
of its special kind there will ever be.
We who find this so penetratingly sweet
in our loving of the earth and of each other
must not let a moment of this glorious day escape.

Celebrate Our Changes

My genetic family, at first seven,
Runs out with me
That need not be the end,
Or birth and death seem both
To be accidental and senseless.
Proven orderly are innumerable
Newly discovered phenomena.
We may go on with our influence
Through our love and teaching.
So may those whom we have served
Do the same, and project
Their influence endlessly.
This type of immortality might be
Brought about by all souls
Of good intent, and others warmed.

By their caring, sometime join in, too.
Each one going on leaves space
And vigor for the living
Of younger ones. We are thankful
For the completion here
Of the living of a useful life,
And may there be a bit
Of merriment to cheer it on.

My Wife, the Cook

Love somehow has grown to be
a most confusing thing, from an
out-of-mind extravagance of feeling
through various stages of insanity
to settling down to complacency
with boredom yet to follow.
I have decided that the matter
must be addressed anew with techniques
I never knew before. Rather than starting
out to hunt for a new mate at my age,
I'll do what can be done to keep the old one
standing by. I can't do anything right,
it seems, but I do enjoy her more
since I have grown so old and deaf.
And what a cook!

My Hope for You

Let there not be sadness when I am gone.
Remember not what I have done or left undone
for that cannot be changed.
Think more of what we've tried to do together
to foster and build loving concern for others
that they may go on serving others too.
You will reach the ones in need
more potently as you grow your own best selves.
Somehow I hope I'll know.
You may sometimes feel a breath of my contentment
and my continuing love.
There should be no end to such as this.

You with Me

It is a warm and greener growing day
and the clouds are big ships
and little ships and puffs and whiffs
of anything you want to see in them,
and I see you in everything good
and beautiful today. There is a feel
of going on. Does it matter where
or for how long? The native grass
upon the hill outside my window
is short and almost within my touch.
It is already spiked with flowering
of buffalo, and heads of gramma grass
unlike any other seed display;
A quietness hangs in the air
and nothing stirs except the trailing green
of deeper hanging bushes in the
swollen stream from melt of
mountain snows. Along the bank
the shaded deeper green
serpentines its way a thousand miles
into the waiting sea.
Is this our journey too, and will we
so go on together,
you with me?

You

The crying years have crawled along without my knowing they have been dead since that long time back when you failed to come home from work at all. Those late afternoons or early evenings as the seasons changed were the high time of all our day, for when you came into our home your eyes lit up and long and clinging was our kiss and your strong, large-holding embrace.

Our gentle evening passed and we were locked into ourselves the whole night long. Then all went dead for me.

And where were you? Or are? The sobbing years have gone on endlessly to drain my very bones of tears that never dull their endless aching.

What happened to you then? Or was it I? The questioning, the search, the lawful and more awful prying press have crucified and tainted most of our old relationships. Our kin have stood close by but in the eyes of some of our sweet neighbors there seems to be a curdling of the cream that once enriched us all.

Many times have I toyed with the resolve to seek a drowning of pain's consciousness, but something stayed my hand from doing it. Nor can I leave our home that must remain a haven yet awhile.

My haunting dream may yet come true. Though I am but a bag of bones might I not once again hear his dear step and see his lit-up eyes as he walks into our home once more?

"Du Bist Die Ruh"

You are my rest
Du bist die Ruh
The music's sweet
The words ring true
If we but sing it
Tho' apart
Our hearts will beat
As just one heart.

"My Heart is on the Wing Today"

My heart is on the wing today
And it may never settle down again
For your beloved voice I thought was lost
Since it was muted for a longer time
Than I could bear, came through the air.
All is singing once again.
The mountain's and the streams rejoice
And humble creatures too are blessed
By just the feel of your sweet presence
Everywhere.

"Emotional Tranquility"

You bring to me again a sense of unity within and power to take off again.
This freshly blooming day must be for renewal first. That is what you
bring to me. The retching sickness of too much strain and fear of failing
those who dreamed up possibilities that were not there, have been living
with me for too long. Now you have come back forcibly in my memory,
and smoothed the hurts, repaired the breaks, and lofted up the hopes
that had been beaten down. A deadness stirs itself to living once again
and you are here. It is enough. There is only now a loving quietness and
you.

"Wanderer"

The pleasant meandering of your heart guides me as well
Who should have walked through fields of flowers in the
Spring and rested in the dappled light of summertime that
Fills with fragrance the senses to exuberance.
Such wanderings of the soul
Now come so late
That I must find a way
To celebrate full life again.
I would that I could wander
Free and farther now.
Oh let me go along with you
Meandering on and on
To where there is no end
Of such content.

"The Day Hangs On"

The day is in a holding pattern
Not knowing whether it is Winter
Or a far too early Spring.
The greening buds have been enclosed
In balls of cotton, coldly holding them
In suspense of waiting.
My heart waits too
As bird caught far from home
Embattled by the swirling storm
Sits underneath the bending down
Of evergreen branches
Overloaded by the snow.
So my old heart bends down
In the loss of you
Too early flown out of your nest
In Summer time.
The longing grows
Till you must feel the pull
Of my yearning
And fly back home again
My lovely one.

"Bird Calling"

My heart is a calling bird
That wants to come back home to you
Who let me go reluctantly
On wings of my longing to be free.
Ambition drove me high, as a falcon flies
Shot through the blackness of the night
With jagged lightning slice of light.
So did I soar aloft on all my dreams
And looked down on the sea's immensity,
Diving down to play with ripples
Born in the Rocky Mountain streams
That flowed a thousand miles to lose themselves
In the turbulence of the open sea.
I dived and laughed at them, they rose
Upon the waves to taunt me and then
Sank down into oblivion and were lost to me.
The years now seems as broken toys that only you
Can mend and then leave behind.
I fancy that you call my name upon the wind,
But dying down again there is no whisper yet.
I call again and yet again into the void
But nothing answers me at all.
But in the darkness of the quiet night
I feel the breath of you upon my cheek
And in the heart of me there comes the pulse
Of your loving, and I hear again your beloved voice
Calling me to fly back home to you.

"Night and Shining Day"

Night time holds us close together
Now at last.
Starshine winds it's fingers
Round us, holding hearts
Close and tender.
Day breaks open eyed.
Sun laughs and wakes us up.
We rise and walk out
In the open day
Needing only to hold hands.

"Love Song Just for You"

I wrote a little verse for you
It was to be a love song too
But words became so envious then
Because the music was so sweet
They got entirely twisted round,
Entangled in their metered feet.
The music quietly withdrew
Wrote tenderly of what it knew.
The love song was more luscious then
A song without a word, or end.

"Passing By"

Everyone's a pal of mine today,
You did not pass me by
As if I were a dried up leaf
Blown past you on the desert wind
Of no coming back again.
You touched me
Lying there in my despair
And drew me up,
To your full height.
The flood of your heart's caring
Soaked into me as summer rain
Renews to greenness
The desert sands again.
Fragrance of flowers goes with me now.
You filled me with your trust
As water swells the dried out sponge
To fuller weight than it can hold
And must spill over
To another one.
So do I touch the others
Passing by,
For all are dear to me
I see you in every one of them.

Bits
and
Pieces

A Breeze Blows Through

Wandering waif of a breeze
In this lightly clouded day,
What do you want of me
Who can go out and dally
Only in my heart?
It may seem strange
In these gaunt years
To yet seize hold
Of gaity and wildness anywhere.
My doors and windows
Are open to all.
There's no restriction
To coming in of those
Who fill my years with joy
So warmly and abundantly.

Limericks

There was a young fellow, Hieronamous
Whose ancestors all were agronamous.
To New York he went
Fame and fortune hell bent,
He came back home broke and anonymous.

"Here lies the body of Mary Ann Lowder
She burst while drinking a sedlitz powder.
Gone from this home
To her heavenly rest,
She should have stayed till it effervesced."

Immigrant Woes

"What a funny bird a frog are
when he hop he flops not
He ain't there almost
Ain't it if but?"

Worry Grinds Down

The gritty taste of worry
grinds down the teeth of trouble
and makes the mind and body
collapse, and discumbobbles
the only life I'll ever know.
But one who's born a vixen
with not a care for others
knows not the fun of fixin'
the problems of the others,
for everybody's likely got
some troubles too.
I'll go on helpin' others,
I've got to go on tryin'
for no one wants to listen
to this old lady's cryin'.
I'd better go lie down
and forget it for awhile.

Odor Eaters

"Don't use odor eaters
Or you'll be gone,"
said a kid to a friend.
What a rancid remark to make!
Let's banish both of them.

Heart Attack?

You can have a heart attack
and take time off from work
to get over it.
So why not take time off
for pleasure first,
and so fore-stall a heart attack
at all?

Mostly Money

Money should be important
mostly when one doesn't have
enough to live decently. Too much
may enslave more than it frees.
Its use is what matters and not
the worship of it as a goal.
This principle may not be accepted
by the dedicated seeker after wealth.
Too few escape that insane race.
Those who do may find serenity
in their souls who offer aid
to those who try to help themselves,
and mercy and non-judgment
toward the losers.
Such should be a worthy reason
for the living of a man.

Verbosity

Verbosity is my disease
I'm told.
Some call it other names
As well.
Argument has been a sin
I was braced up to defend.
Cacaphony of words and sounds
Have done me in.
Friends have warned me
But worn out with failure,
Have gone away
Unheeded.
If I renounce them now
For their stance
Then will my enemies
Fold in
To claim me
As their prey.
Must I give in
To foe at last?
Or yield to love
That knocks me down
But then holds out
Its hands
To lift me up again?

Simplicity is rubbed
Into the wounds
Of my own making.
Sparcity shall be
My guiding light.
One word for two
Or five or ten,
A leaner diet—
But oh the joy
Of having time
To listen to another's words!

Cutting It Short

I was told when writing verse
to make it as long as I liked
then cut it down to half,
then amputate it once again
and so on till it was
as skimpy as my thinking.
I started with a noble horse,
a dog, a cat, a rat, a mouse,
a louse, and now
it is a flea.
Alas! just see what this
has done to me.

Why Did We Marry?

You are the most exasperating man
I've ever known
and yet I cannot let you go alone.
The house is empty since the kids are gone
and now you want the freedom
just to frolic on your own.
I wonder how much better
would have been the end
if it had been a temporary liaison?

The Fight Goes On

From the dark recesses of my moral past
what devious frolicking has occurred to me?
Is it merely a dying spasm of regret
that I must be the last leaf
on the otherwise bare tree
that goes into its winter,
sparse of color, splash, and potency?
Can this be I who dares to make
these utterly insane remarks?
Or is this someone else
inside of me?

A Step Up

When you defer to me
and think me better than I am
I strain to reach to level
of your view,
then find that you have grown
to be a wiser man
but once again
You lift me up with you.

Tit for Tat

What matters in the end
that there is trouble
off and on,
If there be love and joy between
and lightful smattering
of fun.

Nice - Vice?

You are perfection
of form and face
with "Figger" any artist
would want to paint,
but are you truly
the saint they say you are?
There is a touch of earth
in your sweating palm
that touches mine in sympathy.
The warm look
in your brown eyes
picks up the beating
of my pulse.
Do I perceive
a hint of levity
in your glance?
And is there
just a touch of vice
perchance?

Quotables from Modest Folks

The best advice I ever had
was when I was in a Catholic school.
Sister said, "You earn an indulgence
every time you make somebody laugh."

Quick interplay of thought
and feeling binds us closer
to any friend.

If you need an excuse to live,
why are you?

You've been through the operation
of the century and now,
next day, you expect
to get up and jump rope.

The Old Reliables

A misanthrope has never seemed
a noble aim, or trend,
to non-approval would I claim,
but I do think with all the people
asking for a job, there might be one
who'd try to do just what I need.
But old and tottering friends
still come and do the best they can
and we share memories
over cups of tea or coffee
in the winter time,
old fashioned lemonade
in the hotter summer days.
But oh the jobs are amply done
so amiably.
They come back every time they're due,
Dependably.

Vexation

Exasperation hits again.
He is my friend
so solid in his loyalty
and yet he vexes me.
Must he be perfect?
Has he asked the same of me?

Indelicate

You say I am indelicate
in what I say to you.
What sensitivity have you shown
to others who are lower in capacity
than you, or so you think?
The very slant of that opinion
makes me close my ears
to anything you say.

The Use of Time

Assignment of importance
to temporary things
robs us of time on this good earth.
How shall we use the rest of it?

Lemonade

The day is one to celebrate.
I may be shaping up to go
where others go too soon or late.
It matters not so much the pain,
let's think of it as lemon juice
and all the merry times we've had
delight that adds the sweetening.
The magic lies in bubbling water
that could be tears, but sparkling bright
gives champagne lift to lemonade.
A picnic in the park till dark
and sleep of long remembering.

What Next?

Keep nagging me if that is what it takes
to make you happy. It is lucky
that I see things in a different way,
for we are tied to one another more
each day this animosity goes on.
Neither of us could stand alone
but the neglect you charge me with
is the freedom that keeps me
coming home at all,
and nag, nag, nagging lets off steam
that otherwise would blow you up.
So let's just go along our stormy way
for yet awhile, and God knows
what will be the end of it.
I'd even now rather take a chance
with you than any other female
I've ever known.
At least you keep me wondering
what comes next!
Surprise is more exciting
than security any time.

It Seems To Me

I'll Get Things Done Today

Planning comes the easiest before getting up.
Some clarity is added by planting
reluctant feet upon the floor.
Robes these days get their sleeves mixed up
more than they used to do, and dragging
is the gait out to the kitchen too.
A laggard breakfast gives some energy
for a while. Now it's not reasonable
to bestir oneself at once, for digestion
needs a quiet time for rumination.
Alas, this ends in a dozing off, for
rest should never be denied the
faithful service of good old stomach.
Now morning is the freshest time
to assemble, through the window,
the plans of Nature for the day as well,
so there we come to ten o'clock.
There are so many hours ahead and what's
a schedule for if not to be altered for more
pressing enterprises that come to mind?
It's time now for a snack to set the juices
running once again, and then 10 minutes
nodding time which somehow hums along
to almost noon. This is all that is now
clear to me, so much just walked inside my door.
There is no energy left today except to take
myself to bed. Ah! Tomorrow! Fresh
young day. I'll rise up early
and get everything all cleared out
most surely then.

TV Guidance

"It's not a crime to grow so old
But it's mighty inconvenient."
Now I'm pushing eighty-eight
And that with me would be just fine
If others didn't emphasize it
By asking me how it feels to be so old.
It feels much better than in those
Nervous, struggling years, when daring
To brace up to competition
Was demanded of younger ones
Instead of a quiet choosing
Of a simple way.
Now I'm incapable of doing much
But watch the drivers seek success
While I lean back and view the sky
And wonder why I ever sought
To reach the stars. Now I can see
The marvels of the firmament
And listen to the sound astir,
And thank the Creator for leaving me
The sense and senses to enjoy
Them all.
"Getting older," said the last good lady,
"Is not a crime. It's a priviledge."

Difference in Language

A man's own native tongue
Must be the sweetest sound to him
As mine is to me.
I honor those who come here
At so much cost to their security.
I have longed to try
Just such a thing myself
But lacked the courage.
What an excitement have I missed.
I am depleted more than they.
I speak slowly and carefully
With too much working of my mouth
And tongue and my heart strains
To hear sounds that interpret them to me.
At last our too hard trying
Collapses as we laugh
And hug each other and share
Whatever food there is around.
We have so much in common
That differences of tongues
Disappear until another time.

Fire and Water

A group assembled on an ocean front
to rehearse a drama of a great many years
of scholarly research and writing, on matters
of the universe and rebuilding attitudes
and life upon this earth.
To light the scene, they piled up driftwood and
kept it burning til almost dawn
when everyone had reached exhaustion.
Many hands dipped up buckets of
ocean water to put out the fire.
Thrown together, the flames and burning
wood shot out, almost burning some
who fled, but were speckled on
their cloths and skin.
The standard thing to put out fires lay all about
loosely, to be scooped up. Their minds
were too far off to see the sand.
Was this an answer to their decades
of crusade or powerful shot of
practicality? Who can answer such a thing as this?
I wager it will only stimulate them futher.
Disaster has a way of doing that.

"Perspective of a Woman"

"Perspective of a woman," that is the spark in this amiable morning that sets me off in a renewed search for meaning in the natural and some-times termed abnormal attachments of human beings of every class and condition. At last the non-generic intellect may calmly deal with all forbidden subjects that may have troubled man since there was one, or at least two.

The universal intellect, or "individual" ones are wakened from the taint of "natural depravity" and horrid persecutions to calmer assessment of the complicated matter.

We are born sexual and there is only glory and no shame in it. Then why is that creative force denied to many who with deepest spiritual service, love and counsel their fellows to the increased flowering of good and vital needs of everyone? Those who are reduced in effectiveness with inner calm are more restricted in their power. They are chained to servitude where there should be righteous and tender joy? What is wrong with us? Who are we to say that freer sexuality is all bad? We do not dwell in ignorance and poverty and unknown bestiality that enslaved people do. Are we fit to judge these others whose only sparking power lies in their in-born sexuality?

All living things are basically fecund and pleasured by their feelings and even the inanimates whisper or roar the stimulating words and songs that magnify the creativity of every breathing thing. Even the unmoving mountains declare the majesty of the Great Creator and the dappled brooks with sensuous and murmurring words and song grow later into the roaring cataracts that sweep with increasing passion into the engorg-ing sea.

Should we not too, in our hearts and souls celebrate and do honor to that great delight of all—the flaming force and reclaiming goodness of our common steaming sexuality. That is what powerfully charges the great-est of our singers, artists, writers, humble men and creatures of the wild in a common sense of feeling and tenderness. It is our soul's salvation and the ineffable delight of our universal sensuality.

Something Bothers You?

Why not take the easy way
Of making out today?
You are not the only one
Who wants to get along
With that irritating neighbor
Just across the way.
Perhaps there's something hurting him;
You're limping too, yourself, I see.
So it's a pebble in your shoe?
Why don't you shake it out?
Now tell me once again
What all your worry is about.

Is There a Past?

There surely is a present
so there must have been a past,
but pain may have caused me
to forget so much of it.
This bright morning of recall
fights its battle to be known
and dealt with once again.
Remembered after many tries
are shadows only of happenings
covered by forgetting all this time.
Old age is kindly treated thus,
I must believe.
I will rise up and put
my house and mind in order,
for new excitement
may walk in today.

Freedom of Belief

Break away from sameness
on this different day.
Time never can stand still,
nor can retreat for long
if there is to be a going on.
The mold of yesterday's beliefs
may not hold in the need
of expanding souls with longing
to be free of all constraints,
and so create somewhat themselves again.
Interpretations are various
as Spring's erratic temperament.
But sober minds may once again
distill their own beliefs
to fit their special needs today.
The source is solid yet.
We draw from that and use it as we need
without restraint of others'
cloying and blind demands.
There is a freedom of choice here
that must belong to every man.

Too Late to Appreciate

Evil is as evil does
and reaps its reward or not
and it is open knowledge.
But good is sometimes quite unknown
except by the one who does it.
The soul of giving knows its own content
before its effort has been spent,
but the joy of giving anonymously
is, to my mind, either timidity
or a form of selfishness,
for those who receive this bounty
do suffer in their minds
from never knowing who cared so much
for them.
A man I knew contrived
his many benefactions so.
Strangely, grieving was left
those mourners after he was gone.
How sad that he had caused
so much of what he had tried
to alleviate.
They had found out who it was too late.

Just Wait and See

The things that children hear
the P.E. big boys say sometimes to bolster
their own courage, it is thought,
come through the open windows on hot days
and sound as if the devil himself
was coaching them to say these ribald things.
And sure enough the children tell them
openly at home and scandalize the mothers
mostly, who are left to deal with this
rank situation. Is it any wonder
that tears come, with anger and frustration
that follows? What would you do,
my old tongue asks of me? I do not
at the moment know, but there were
problems in my time that were even harder
to solve. It is a bed of fire through which
the modern parents walk, and anger
only drives the children's confidence underground.
The voice will not easily be soft,
and answers slow and conversational,
unless they have the patience of a Job,
and insight of a Socrates.
My country school was but one room
with seldom more than eleven kids,
and everyone had heard and seen
all the natural earthy things. So I don't know
what I would do today. It might be
my great grandchild coming home
from school and my grandchild counselling her.
And this old addled soul
might just have given up
and gone to bed.
Whatever is done in gentleness
and love will surely turn out well
in the end, but there might be
a lot of waiting in between.

I Have Been Too Rigid

Relentless comes the nearing end
of emotions kept restrained
for all these years, on demand
of sturdy righteousness.
I have not wanted this to be
and now, almost too late,
I would go out upon the earth
and feel the pulsing drive of it
and lie enfolded there perhaps
by one who has been halfway dead
as I have been these many
desiccated years. I would rather
have my Heaven now
if I am forced to make a choice.
I will not leave before I know
what has made so many others
choose to die for the losing of it.
And if I miss a future Heaven,
perhaps this lovely one on earth
may be enough.

Repetitious

A story that appeals to me
is repeated many times.
You will bear with me, I hope.
I am not dumb
but forgetful and repetitious.
I've wondered earlier
what made many of the old,
not all,
go over endlessly
the recollections of long ago.
Now I understand and do the same
often with tears flowing in streams.
It is not for your entertainment, friend,
but because I feel at ease with you.
I must recall in greater detail
what I needed earlier to forget
for saving of my self respect.
The tears are for the moistening
of my heart
that might grow sere and unfeeling
save for this watering.
Your long suffering and good cheer
have brought back once again
the sunlight of my going on.
I wish I could remember
not to do this any more.

Breakfast Time

I sink my teeth into life today,
and ruminate as I
savor every morsel.
Motionless are the trees in
the barely moving air.
It is a remote and quiet
place. There promises to be no
sun before night comes.
All need to look into the
future has vanished with the
richness of this time when
all the loved ones gone
before seem to have returned and
are breathing here again.
The universe itself is
settled down at ease
with nothing more to be
desired than this one
quiet meditating day.

A Day of Accounting

The unresolved but sleeping past
and unknown future
separate themselves by just today.
My age commends me
to a quiet thinking pace.
What complications can be satisfied?
As little time as possible
may be spent concerning things
that cannot be helped, except
for words of sorrow for the sad.
A sparking of confidence
in working ones of good intent
and listening to others' need
just to be heard.
What better way to start this
opening of a bright and spicy
day of spring?

Friends Walk In

The door opens in. Outside there stands a sign
asking all to ring and walk inside,
a very simple thing that should bring
no comment, yet there are those
who question this deeming it unsafe.
For whom? I have not yet bit anyone
nor have others me except in fun.
A cat crept in one time
and jumped upon my bed
surprising only herself.
She had been yowling round the house
before. Once a big old dog
walked all around inside.
I heard his toe nails softly
clipping on the vinyl floor,
going round about before he
found me in bedroom almost
napping. Standing over me
he breathed into my face.
We were friends. Why should I close
my door and turn such visitors away?
There is but one of me to hurt.
But what a host of friends
would I be shutting out.

A Better Crucifixion

Oh, Jesus, all alone in that old tomb,
and sealed in all that dark
with that great rock.
How did You feel? But then
You knew that You would live again.
Would you have gone through that
if You had known what horrors
have been done in Your sweet name?
I wonder what You'd do
if ever You come back again.
Will it be the same?
Who would persecute You now,
Majority or minority?
And would you this time,
after many years in jail,
be strapped in an electric chair?
We do things more humanely now,
in these enlightened days.

Animals May Win Out Yet

Fresh and clear in morning light
the high ridged Great Divide thrusts up
its Rocky Mountain peaks with clefts between
of deeper purple against the light blue
of the morning sky. The sun strikes fire
on bald Pikes Peak and spreads its light
down the slopes to wake the valleys
reaching out as far as eye can see.
Our land is so divided East from West,
but must we humans be the same?
We might better be as normal as the lesser
animals, which somehow get along
if they are left alone. I wonder how
they did it before man multiplied
and took command. Distracting violence
is the order of the day with governance
by those deemed most intelligent. Nature
quietly moves in here and there
and lesser animals may sometime
recover what man, because of greed,
has finally lost.

Different Points of View

Some folks are so modest they feel they are ingrown if they consider seriously their own health at all, while others go to ultra depths of imagined misery to make themselves out as exceptional victims to be pitied and helped.

If they could be thrown together in a gunny sack of ample size and turned and twisted by the enclosed doubts and major catastrophies therein for a goodly length of mixing time, it's no telling what the result might be.

Perhaps such bedrock therapy would change the lives of all of them somewhat. Even that would be some better than no change at all.

The Christmas Spirit

Christmas, Nineteen Eighty-Six, an idle youth, an extra fix!

More money given by parents, just to spend and buy their heir's approval thus.

What is wrong with them instead?

Who robbed them of their self-esteem and confidence and makes them pass along this frantic insecurity and need for approbation from this once innocent generation?

We have claimed the Christmas Spirit as a partner in all this. Is this what that Man of God or godly man taught and personified? He must be deeply grieved at what is done in celebration of His birth at Christmas time.

Questions of Morality

Purity and innocence somehow sound impossible to me even when applied to the young and inexperienced ones. For if a child is sinner from his birth, as some are thought to believe, then must his birthing be considered fouled though consecrated by religious ceremony more than nine months previous.

Sometimes I wonder if the fears that bred these stern beliefs and grave pronouncements were but the flagellation of the guilty and forboding ones who from their inability to cope passed sin on to their descendents.

Can we not begin with just our human instincts labled neither good nor bad and live in decent conformity with others of our kind?

If we do no harm to one another and touch lovingly and help all we can, that down-to-earth morality is good enough for me.

The Job of Living

We have a basic job to do that should be simple to accept if not to perform. It is called Living.

Except for handicaps, genetic or accidental, we should be equal in our opportunities but there the trouble starts. Enormous handicaps block the development of some, while overzealous prodding damages others in strange ways. This is not our fault and we had better muddle through the best we can until we are mature enough to take over the control of ourselves.

We may lie down in self-pity and be a burden to others all our lives or pick ourselves up by the scruff of our necks and stand erect as any other man and go along our self-reliant way.

Inequality of birth or treatment may never be overcome. It is not fair to judge those who fail, but too much pampering can be just as damaging. We can give up and so lose the only chance we may ever have to become what we could be.

But we could leave the past behind and take on the job of caring for ourselves and then on the job of helping others too. Life throws down its glove. It is for us to decide if we will pick it up.

Unusual Business Opportunity

"Unusual Business Opportunity" or words so translated by my groping brain. Strange that it should strike me with what I considered a begging attitude when I was young.

But now again the thought comes back in Bible words which I first heard in my home when I was but a child.

"Ask and you shall receive," a simple statement indeed.

It seemed all right for those who interpreted refusals as well deserved. It was a chancy thing.

Now after all those years of business dealing with fairness desired but profit needed, this sharp reminder has shocked me with its human possibilities. If you give me of yourself or what you can spare, I feel that I must give out with at least an increase of living cost to another one who needs what I can give, and he and others may continue with this exciting game.

My calculator or computer or sophisticated machinery is not programmed for such as this. There are those patient and enriched ones who still use the reliable old abacus. I may go back and plan my attitude again. It is more practical to enjoy this kind of treasure here on earth than store it up in a distant and perhaps uncertain Heaven.

Beyond

There have been times in the long gone past
When I'd have traded all the later years
For painless present, and was tempted to do so
Had not elemental yearning stayed my hand.
It seemed so easy then to go to sleep.

But when the agony of broken bones, along with heartbreak too,
Anesthetized somewhat the pain itself, my longing grew
To live still longer lest I miss the most
Ecstatic thought of all: What lies beyond
The river's bend, or reaches of the sky?

Only then the porous bony structure
Resolved to do a little better job for me.

But I was careful too and my high bed
And old wheel chair have helped me lovingly.

Every morning from my window I see
Visions that have been beyond my dreaming.

I *must* be here to welcome in that day
Of new beginnings. Then I will lie me down
Most gratefully, I hope, for those good years,
And live on in the ones whom I have loved.
And who shall say I may not live again?

Where Freedom Lives

Old age should be where freedom lives. Sometimes it has been earned by working for the right to it by everyone. It seems somehow to be a mantle draped around the shoulders of the aged as manna drifts from Heaven for their nourishment.

Perhaps it has been earned by ardent and painful struggles for the rights of all others too, but often seems to enfold old age in tenderness for no apparent reason at all.

I only know we are bound in chains until our fellow men are struck free too. I would that we could trade places with the young for quite a time. They seem to yearn to grow up and yet dread growing old. How much joy we older ones might have if we could live our youth again and such fire and nobility.

We might want to linger overlong and miss the later better years. But oh the richness the young might experience while they are most active and alive. Perhaps they might catch the more mellow light of understanding that softens fear of growing old and dread of death. When antiquity makes ideosyncracies overlooked, then inner freedom comes in fullest degree.

Old age in many ways is the sweetest time of all.

Christmas

Extravagance, excesses, exhaustion to celebrate the birthday of a Babe, born to humble parents with the shepherds and their animals gathered round in the starshine of open air.

I cannot believe that we have so lost remembrance of the quiet dedication of so simple and so loving a life. Do not count me in on this gaudy display.

It would be more to His liking, I believe, to serve those needy ones He loved the most, and sit down to partake of their plain food enriched with joy of living for others' good.

Perhaps He might come into our own hearts and homes as he did then, if we would leave wide open our own stable doors.

At Christmas

It's a pain to go on doubting.
It's an agony to hate.
It's a hollowness of thinking
To belittle and berate.

If we could know the horror
Of the drubbings others give
Maybe we would judge them better,
Be more willing to forgive.

For they have been the victims
Often hurt by their own sin.
Must we so condemn them
Without knowing what's within?

The misbegotten ones we see
And walk by with a glance
Might not we be the sinners,
They holier than we perchance?

Facts

I have lived with facts too long, too long.
But poetry walked in on the first day of Spring
and broke me loose to live with dreams again.
I am not held inside if I do not choose to be.
Now morning sun stirs to breathing in
the smells of earth and animals
and roving evergreens that quietly
walk down the mountain side
to celebrate with birds, the breeze
and running river down below.
I will gather up my dreams
into reality and walk out to frolic
with the earthy things again.

The lesser intellect
driven by Good Will
may sometimes overleap
the ego centered genius
who only dreams
before his light goes out.

Internal Warfare

The wars of almost a century have gone on
inside of me, and tend to settle down to
rumbling feuds less violent but troubling still.
It has gone on too long, more savage and
destroying in the younger years, at intervals
almost comatose then flaring up in remote
areas blasting wide the morality on which
I once stood firm. Now drawn on too long,
my seventy seven year long conflict is
reduced to pot-shots now and then and
early turbulence may soon be wiped out
by the levelling of passionate involvements
and the drawing in and sealing of the
earthquake schisms to decent
measure of accommodation. (or levelness or quiet?)
We are beginning to make out better,
internal strife and I. Perhaps, just
possibly, peace will be declared
and signed before I die.

Spirit in the Night

Sometime in the sleeping night
my spirit is released
and goes about
and lives its own free life.
Morning brings such change
in what I feel
it could not come
from simple resting
through the night.
Body gives out sooner
with the added years
and mind grows slower
in remembering,
but spirit dances on ahead
when morning light
breaks up the covering
of the night.

This Day Alone Is Gone

The touch of a voice
the feel of a song,
the hearing of birds
on telephone line.
It takes me back
to olden times,
the taste of country
beans with ham
simmered hours
on the old cook stove.
What does it mean to remember this
so pointedly, so hurting-sweet?
The old bones cease their aching
at the touch of loving hands.
I go to bed
but not for long.
I must be fresh
to wake the dawn.

There's Singing in the Air

Too slow you crawled along your sorrowing way,
You endless years since my last family member
Died, and some as dear as were my kin.
A need to be done with all this weakness
Has set in. The start of my faster journey
Has begun. It is not as dreadful
As I thought. Birds sing, flowers bloom
And the country-side, unvisited before,
Seems to draw me easier along.
I feel the old familiar touch of hands
That cared for me, and country smells
Breeze heartily by. The sounds
Of prairie songs now I understand,
The talk of insects intrigues me
And the rush of powerful wings
Ruffles my thinning hair. Oh, there is
A going on, somewhere, somehow.
The call of life is everywhere and you,
So dear, who stay behind, may hear
A sound of tender laughter of content.
Oh, there will come a wondrous melody
Our love has made, and singing will be heard.
I will still be here. It is a tender
And a comfortable touching that we share.